BRAINS

BRAINS

BRAINS

Peter Kagel

Ballantine Books • New York

Library of Congress Catalog Card Number: 88-91984

ISBN: 0-345-35813-9

Cover design by Dale Fiorillo

Manufactured in the United States of America
First Editon: January 1989
10 9 8 7 6 5 4 3 2 1

CONTENTS

INTRODUCTION

On regular occasions it's important to fall back, look around and see the forest for the trees.

And when you do, you come to the realization that we are just comical, greedy, power-hungry, sexually frustrated, lazy animals caught up in an inefficient division of labor. We're basically just rats in a maze. Some rats are smarter than others, but rats nonetheless.

Since mankind is interdependent, you are going to get caught in the maze sooner or later, or, if you are not very wise, forever.

Dissected in this book are the mazes and how they are usually negotiated. Some of them require sophistication, others are traversed dishonestly. Some of them are traps like having to live by the commute or being at the mercy of a lawyer. Some of them are played hypocritically like the politician and TV evangelist.

Treat this book as a road map to life. Remember, the purpose of life is to have fun no matter which maze you have to deal with. Laughing is the grease of life so slide along with me a while and explore our so called "enlightened society."

AN ACCOUNTANT'S BRAIN
[LEFT LOBE]

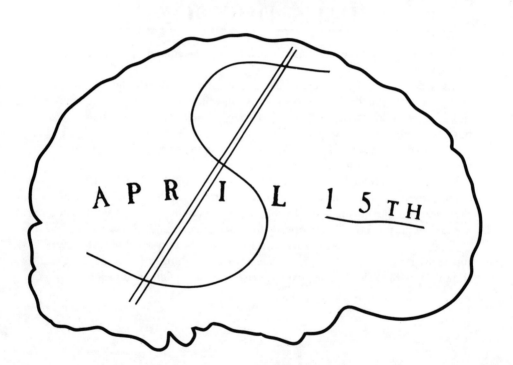

AN ACCOUNTANT'S BRAIN
[RIGHT LOBE]

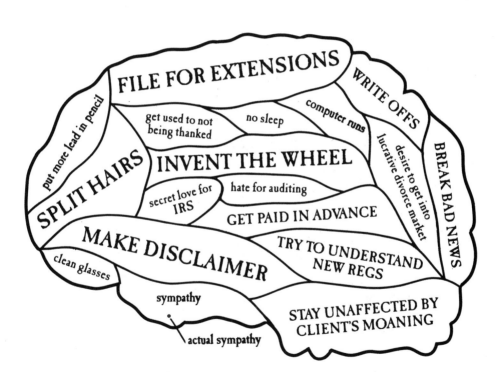

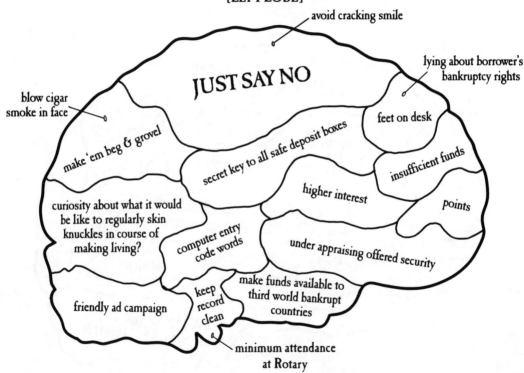

A BANKER'S BRAIN
[RIGHT LOBE]

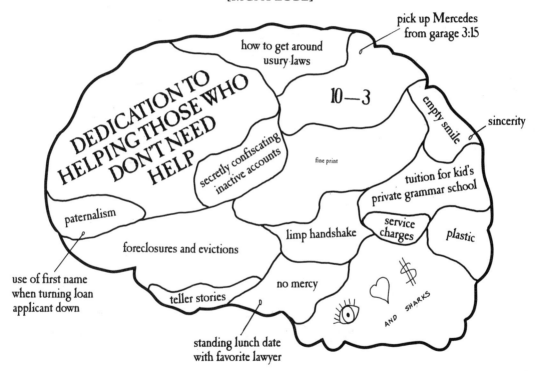

A BARTENDER'S BRAIN
[LEFT LOBE]

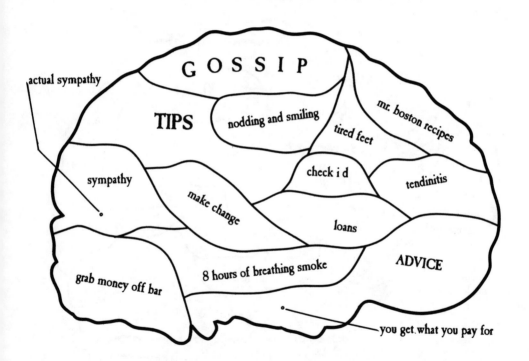

A BARTENDER'S BRAIN
[RIGHT LOBE]

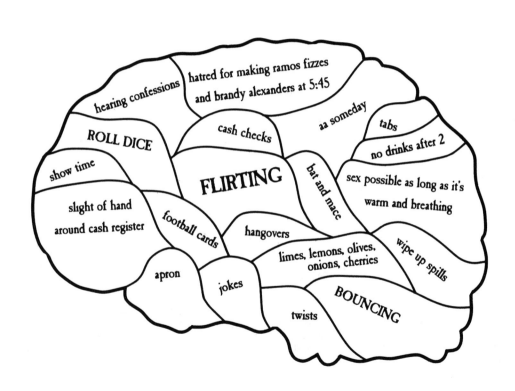

A BASEBALL PLAYER'S BRAIN
[LEFT LOBE]

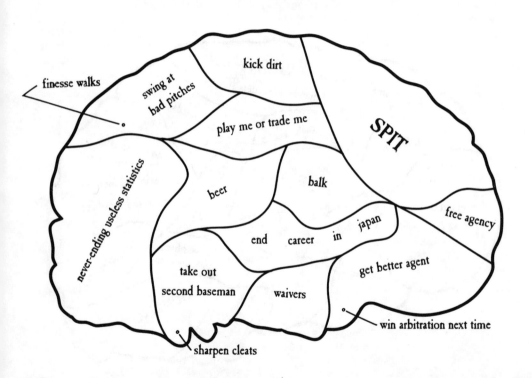

A BASEBALL PLAYER'S BRAIN
[RIGHT LOBE]

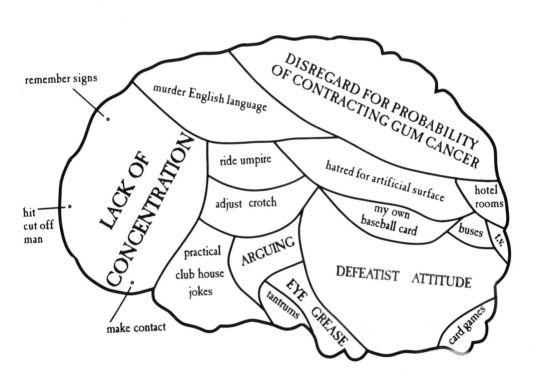

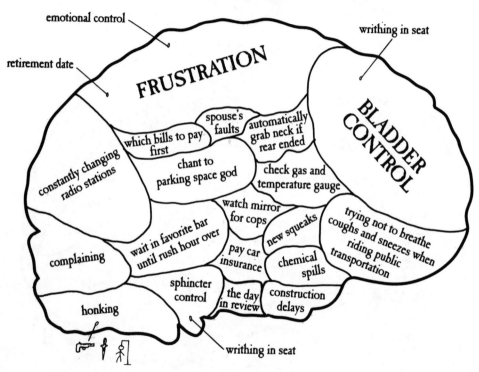

A COMMUTER'S BRAIN
[RIGHT LOBE]

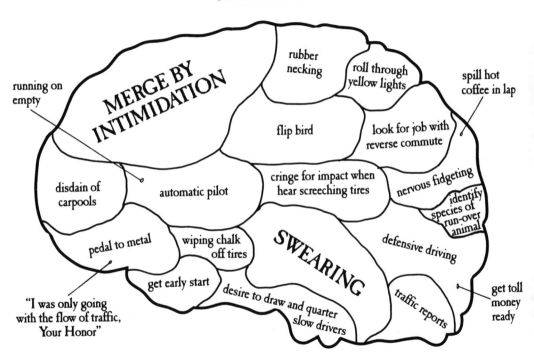

A CONTRACTOR'S BRAIN
[LEFT LOBE]

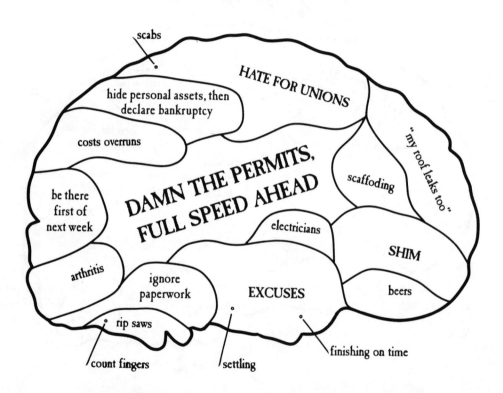

A CONTRACTOR'S BRAIN
[RIGHT LOBE]

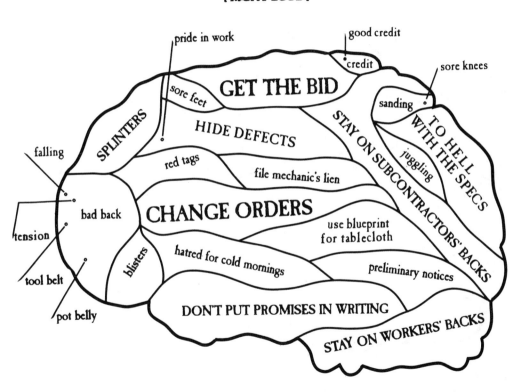

A COUCH POTATO'S BRAIN

[LEFT LOBE]

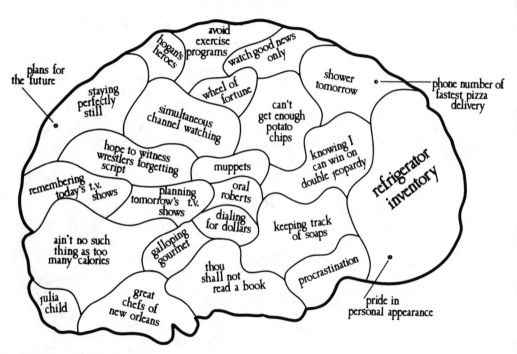

A COUCH POTATO'S BRAIN

[RIGHT LOBE]

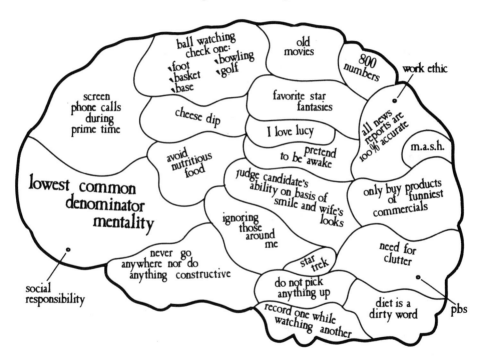

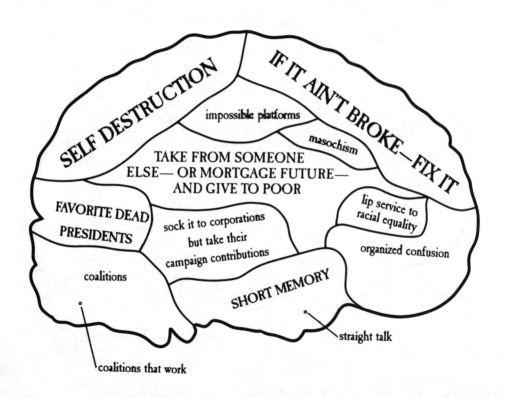

A DEMOCRAT'S BRAIN
[RIGHT LOBE]

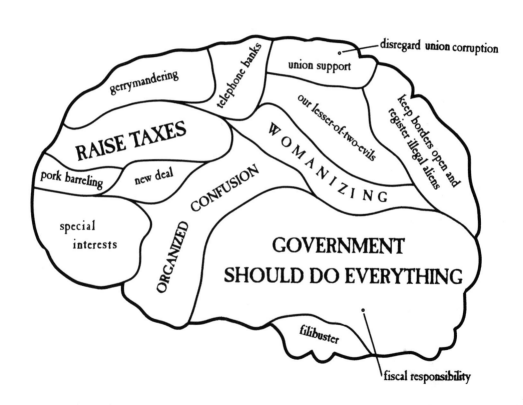

A DIETER'S BRAIN
[LEFT LOBE]

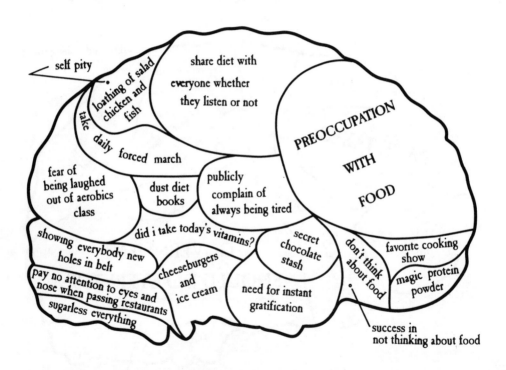

A DOCTOR'S BRAIN

(RIGHT LOBE)

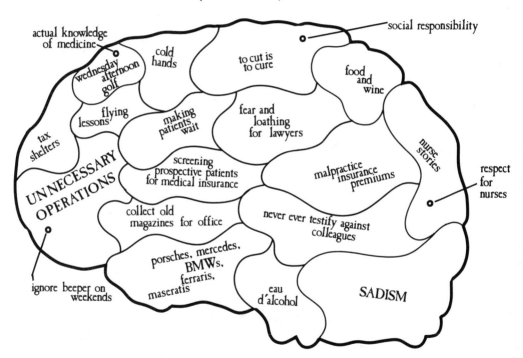

AN EXECUTIVE'S BRAIN
[LEFT LOBE]

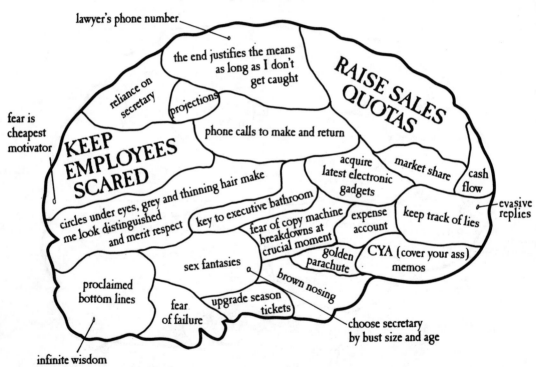

lawyer's phone number

the end justifies the means as long as I don't get caught

RAISE SALES QUOTAS

reliance on secretary

projections

fear is cheapest motivator

KEEP EMPLOYEES SCARED

phone calls to make and return

acquire latest electronic gadgets

market share

cash flow

circles under eyes, grey and thinning hair make me look distinguished and merit respect

key to executive bathroom

fear of copy machine breakdowns at crucial moment

expense account

keep track of lies

evasive replies

proclaimed bottom lines

sex fantasies

golden parachute

CYA (cover your ass) memos

brown nosing

fear of failure

upgrade season tickets

choose secretary by bust size and age

infinite wisdom

AN EXECUTIVE'S BRAIN
[RIGHT LOBE]

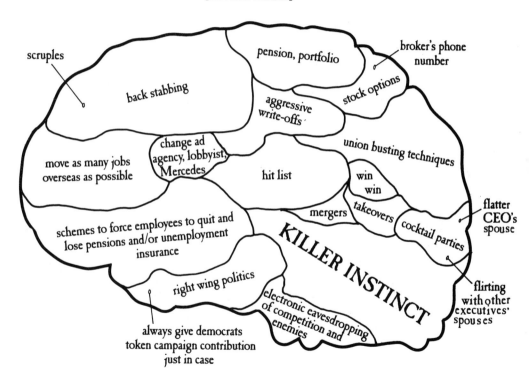

A FISHERMAN'S BRAIN
(LEFT LOBE)

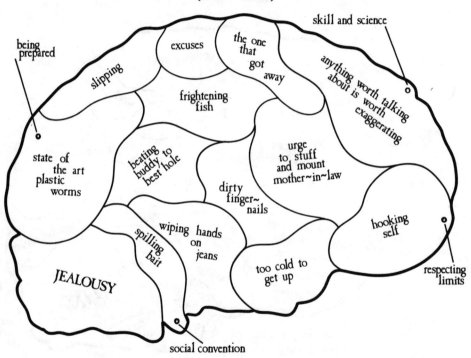

A FISHERMAN'S BRAIN
(RIGHT LOBE)

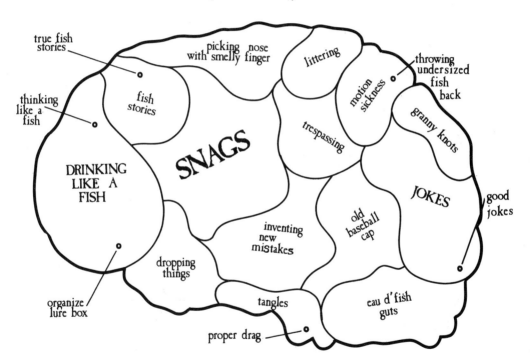

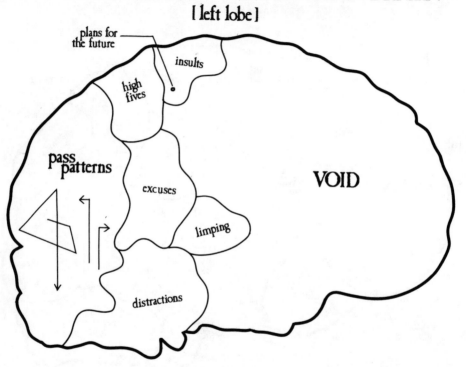

A FOOTBALL PLAYER'S BRAIN
[left lobe]

plans for the future

insults

high fives

pass patterns

excuses

VOID

limping

distractions

A FOOTBALL PLAYER'S BRAIN
[right lobe]

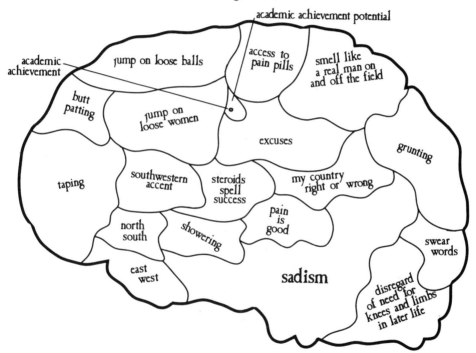

A FUNERAL DIRECTOR'S BRAIN
[LEFT LOBE]

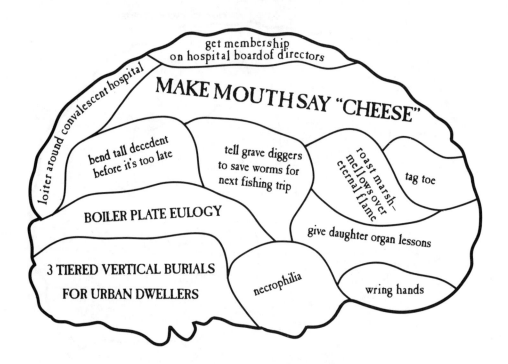

A FUNERAL DIRECTOR'S BRAIN
[RIGHT LOBE]

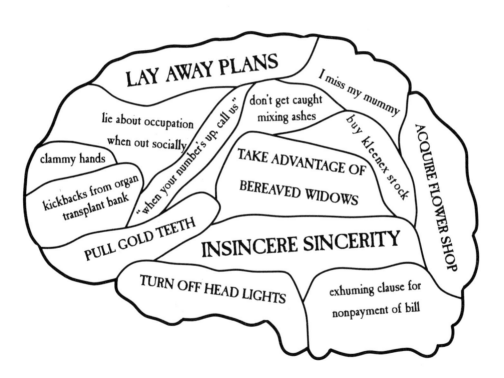

A GAMBLER'S BRAIN
[LEFT LOBE]

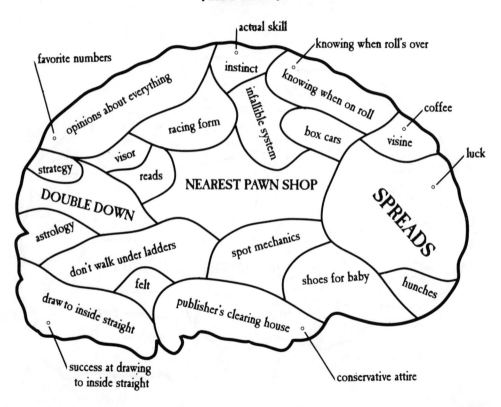

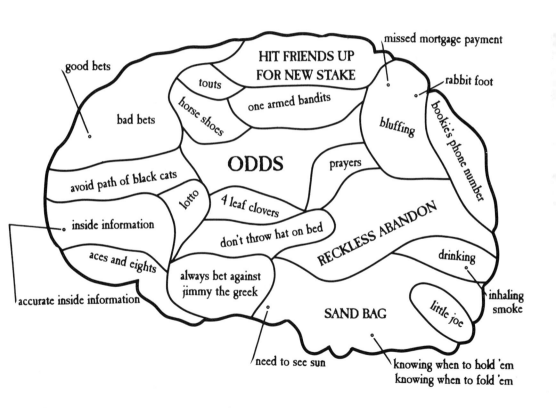

A GAMBLER'S BRAIN
[RIGHT LOBE]

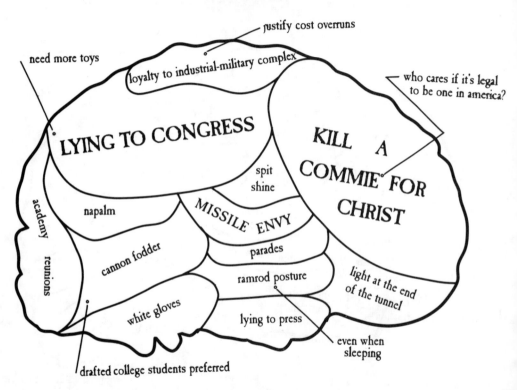

A GENERAL'S BRAIN
[RIGHT LOBE]

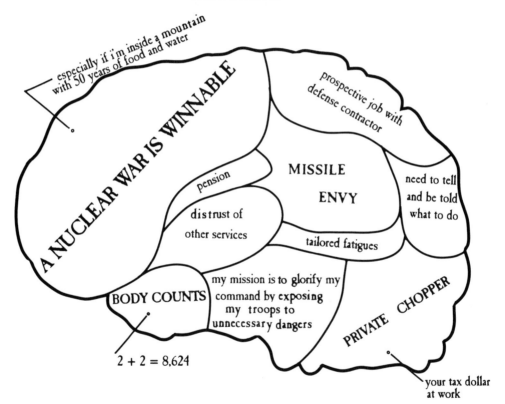

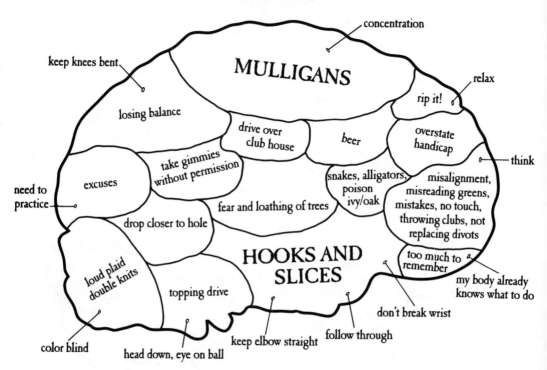

A GOLFER'S BRAIN

[RIGHT LOBE]

drive for show, putt for dough

everybody deserves a sporting chance

being humble in victory

19TH HOLE

yell "fore!" at last possible second

choking

what's a wife for, anyway?

rolling dice for drinks

3 putt greens

lose new balls, find old balls

forget wearing spikes when enter house

subtly distracting opponent

hole-in-one fantasy

on the beach again

give up keeping score

track multi on-going bets

playing through old ladies of both sexes

close deal

lack of confidence

cart races

THINKING DURING BACK SWING

positive visualization

I'm here for the exercise

I'm here to relax

A GOURMET'S BRAIN
[LEFT LOBE]

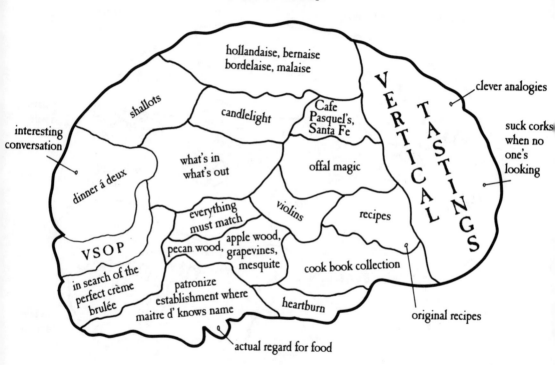

A GOURMET'S BRAIN
[RIGHT LOBE]

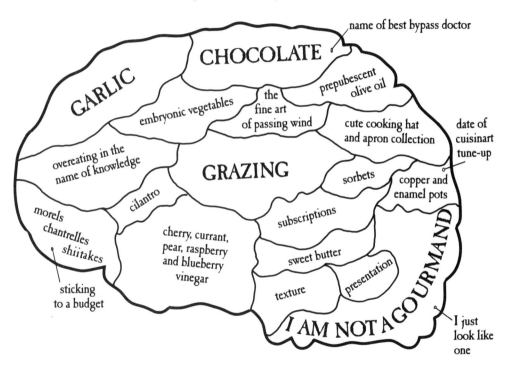

A HACKER'S BRAIN
[LEFT LOBE]

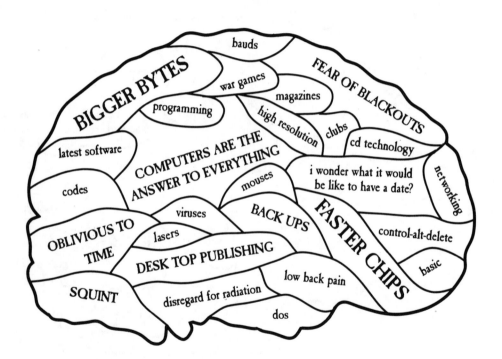

A HACKER'S BRAIN
[RIGHT LOBE]

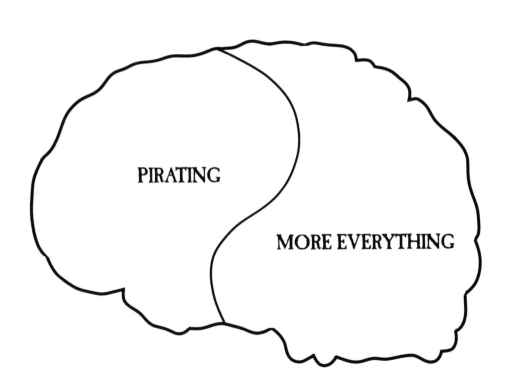

PIRATING

MORE EVERYTHING

A HOUSEWIFE'S BRAIN
[LEFT LOBE]

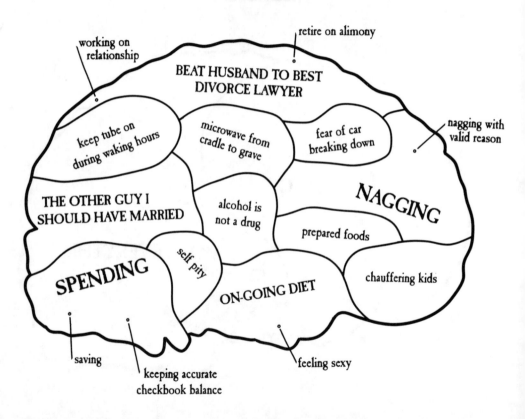

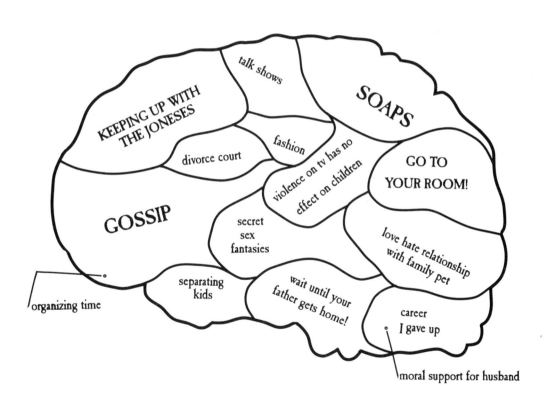

A LAWYER'S BRAIN
(LEFT LOBE)

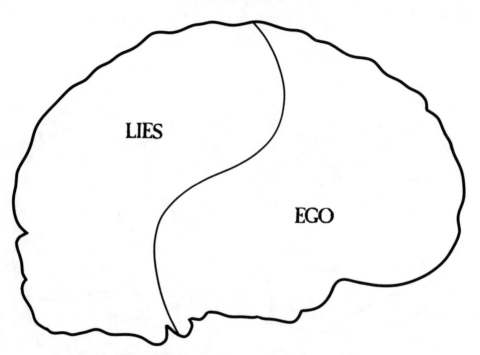

A LAWYER'S BRAIN

[RIGHT LOBE]

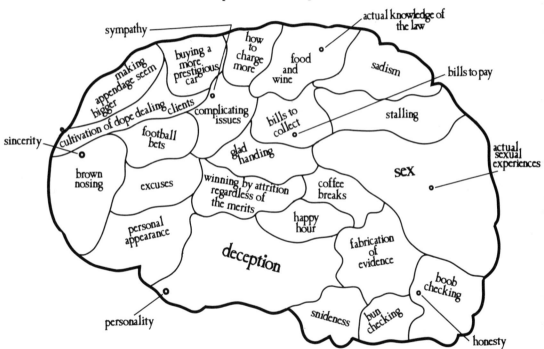

A MECHANIC'S BRAIN
[LEFT LOBE]

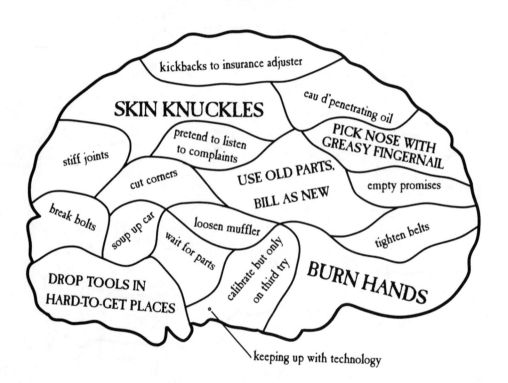

A MECHANIC'S BRAIN
[RIGHT LOBE]

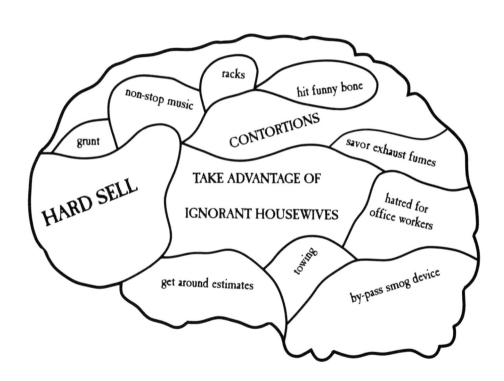

A POLICE OFFICER'S BRAIN
[LEFT LOBE]

A POLICE OFFICER'S BRAIN
[RIGHT LOBE]

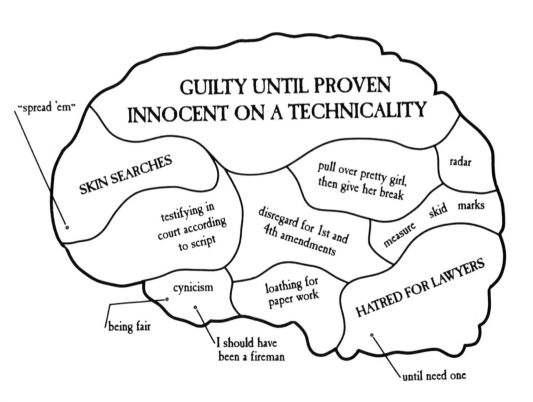

A POLITICIAN'S BRAIN

(LEFT LOBE)

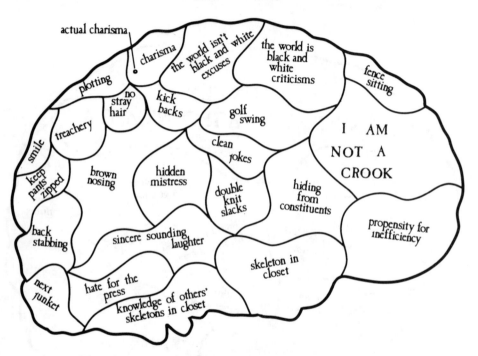

A POLITICIAN'S BRAIN

[RIGHT LOBE]

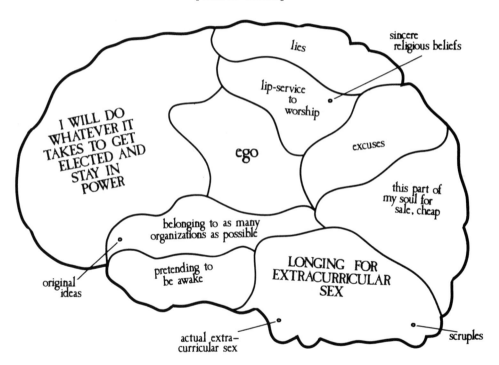

A PSYCHIATRIST'S BRAIN
[LEFT LOBE]

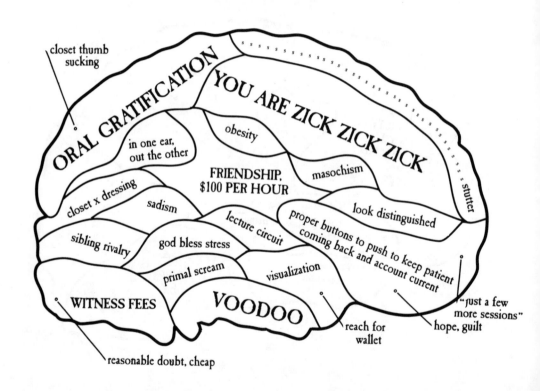

closet thumb sucking

ORAL GRATIFICATION

YOU ARE ZICK ZICK ZICK

in one ear, out the other

obesity

FRIENDSHIP, $100 PER HOUR

masochism

closet x dressing

sadism

look distinguished

sibling rivalry

lecture circuit

proper buttons to push to keep patient coming back and account current

god bless stress

primal scream

visualization

WITNESS FEES

VOODOO

stutter

"just a few more sessions"

hope, guilt

reach for wallet

reasonable doubt, cheap

A PSYCHIATRIST'S BRAIN
[RIGHT LOBE]

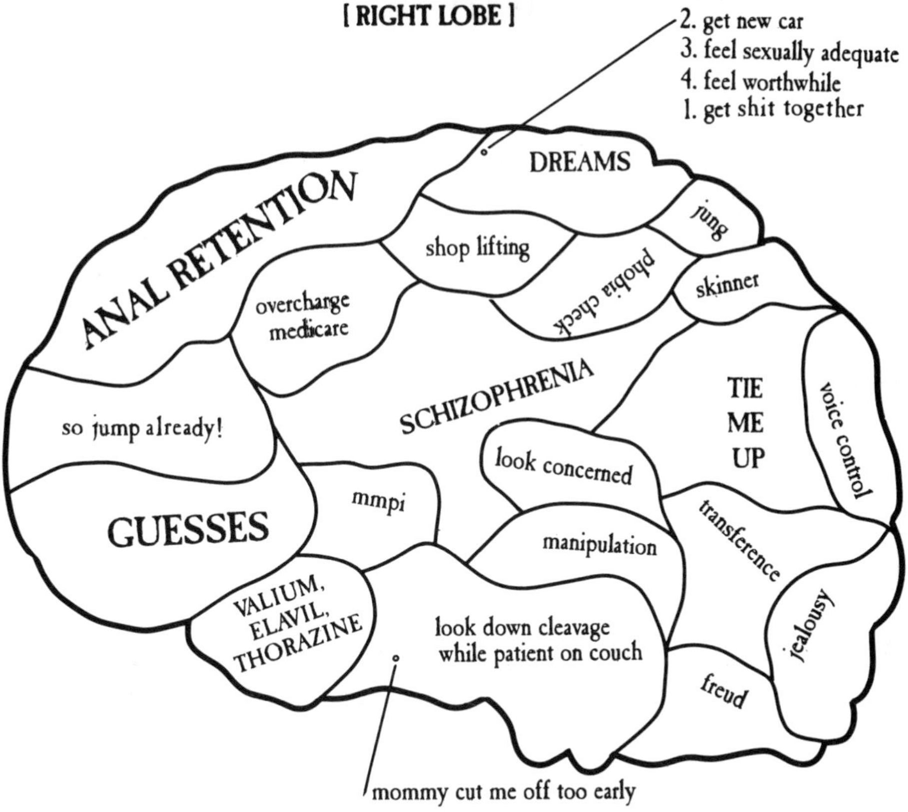

2. get new car
3. feel sexually adequate
4. feel worthwhile
1. get shit together

DREAMS

ANAL RETENTION

shop lifting

jung

overcharge medicare

phobia check

skinner

so jump already!

SCHIZOPHRENIA

TIE ME UP

voice control

GUESSES

mmpi

look concerned

manipulation

transference

VALIUM, ELAVIL, THORAZINE

look down cleavage while patient on couch

freud

jealousy

mommy cut me off too early

A REALTOR'S BRAIN
[LEFT LOBE]

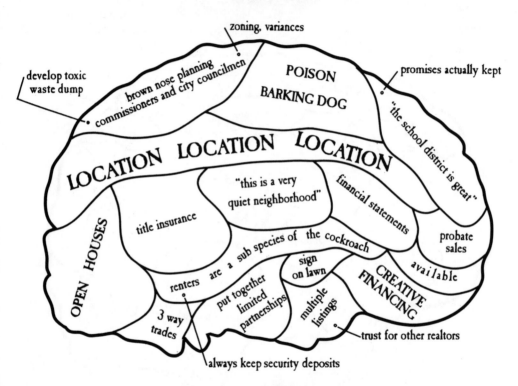

A REALTOR'S BRAIN
[RIGHT LOBE]

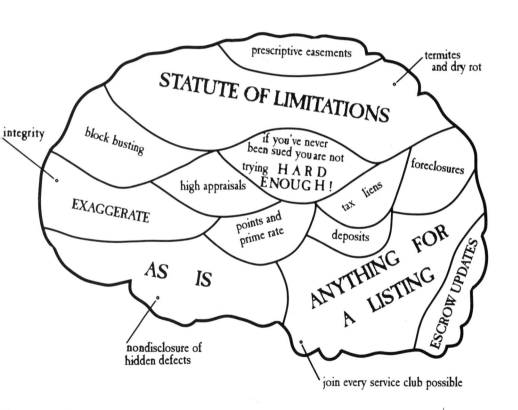

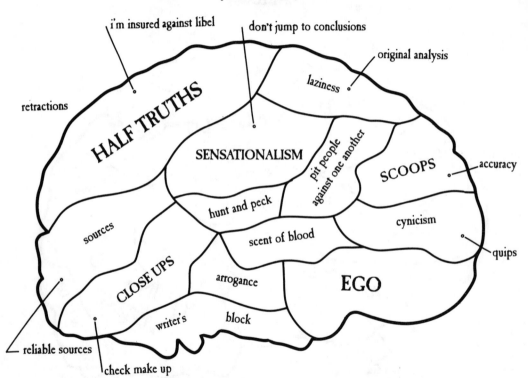

A REPORTER'S BRAIN
[RIGHT LOBE]

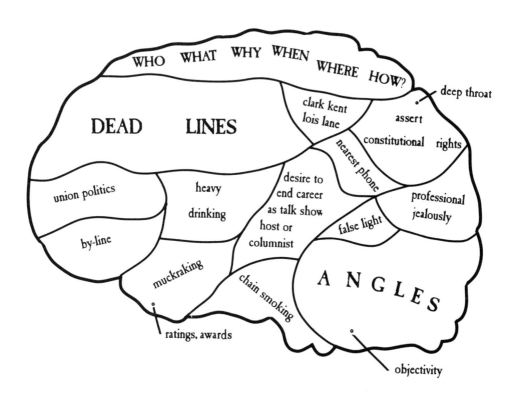

A REPUBLICAN'S BRAIN
[LEFT LOBE]

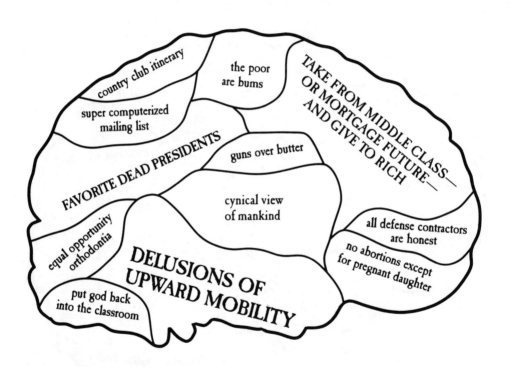

A REPUBLICAN'S BRAIN
[RIGHT LOBE]

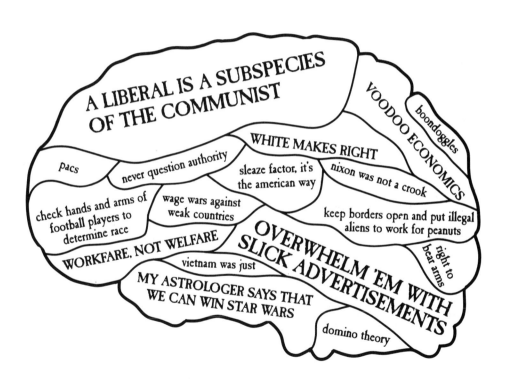

A ROCK MUSICIAN'S BRAIN
[LEFT LOBE]

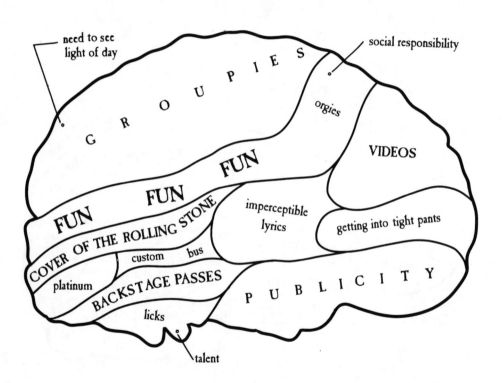

A ROCK MUSICIAN'S BRAIN
[RIGHT LOBE]

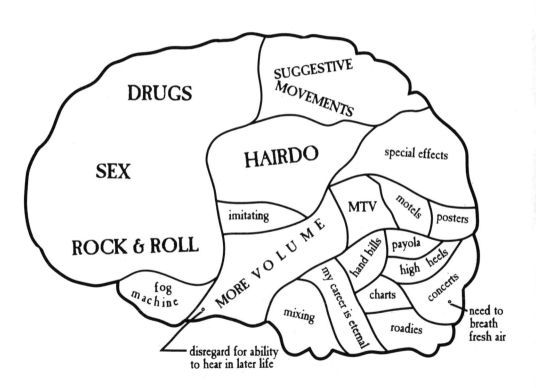

A QUITTING SMOKER'S BRAIN
[LEFT LOBE]

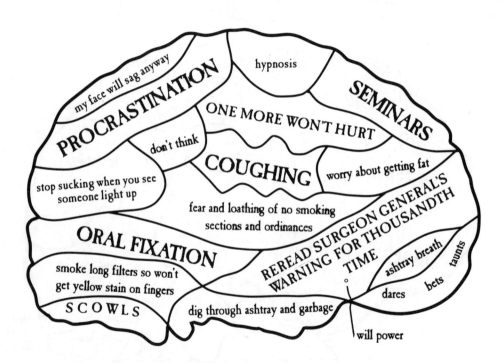

A QUITTING SMOKER'S BRAIN
[RIGHT LOBE]

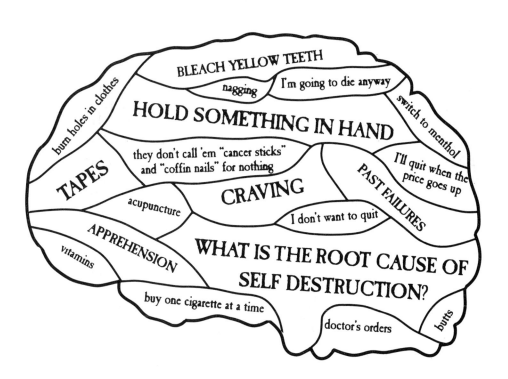

A SECRETARY'S BRAIN
[LEFT LOBE]

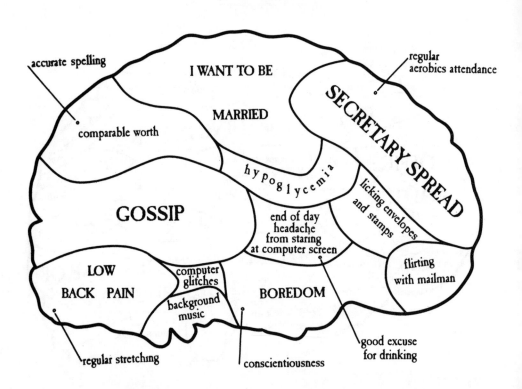

A SECRETARY'S BRAIN
[RIGHT LOBE]

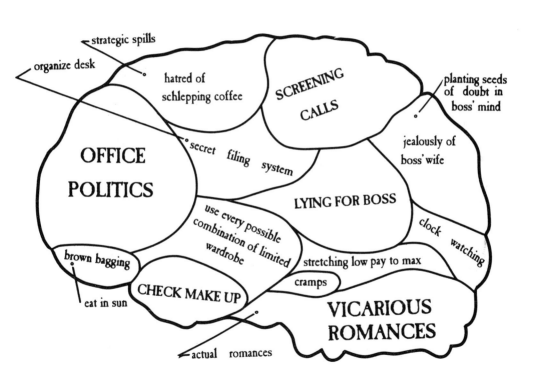

A STUDENT'S BRAIN
(LEFT LOBE)

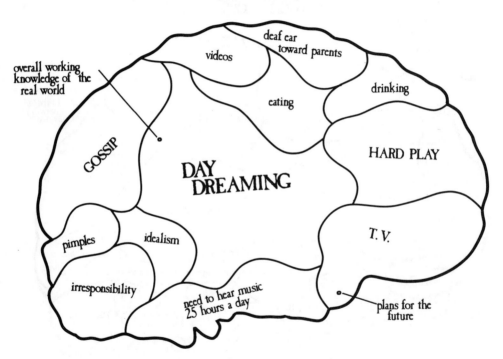

A STUDENT'S BRAIN

(RIGHT LOBE)

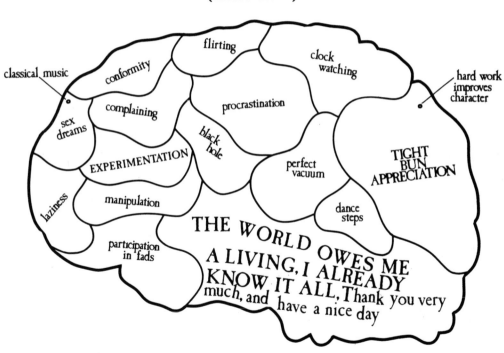

A TAXI CAB DRIVER'S BRAIN
[LEFT LOBE]

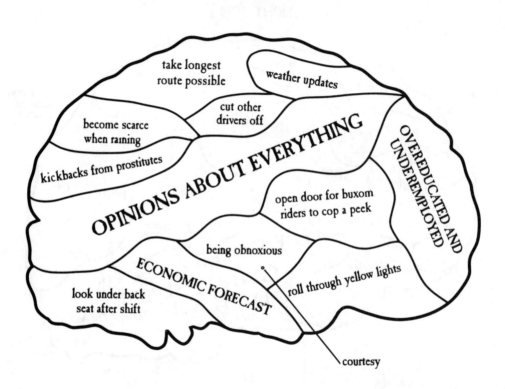

A TAXI CAB DRIVER'S BRAIN
[RIGHT LOBE]

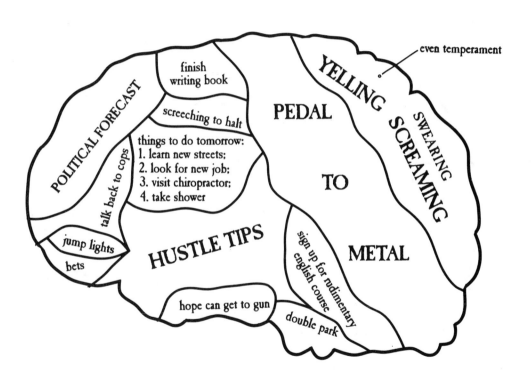

A TEACHER'S BRAIN
[LEFT LOBE]

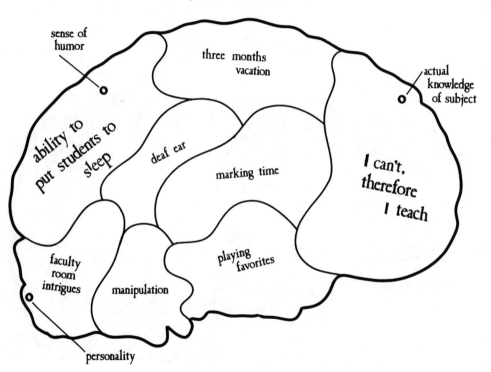

A TEACHER'S BRAIN
[RIGHT LOBE]

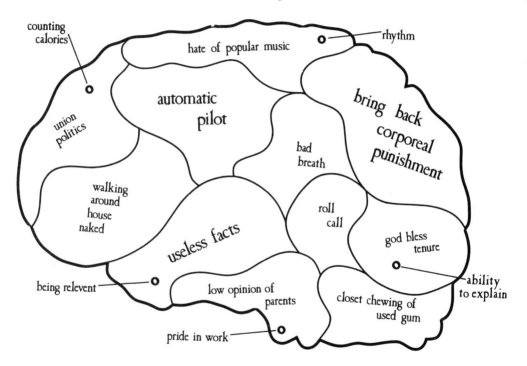

A TELEVISION PERSONALITY'S BRAIN
[LEFT LOBE]

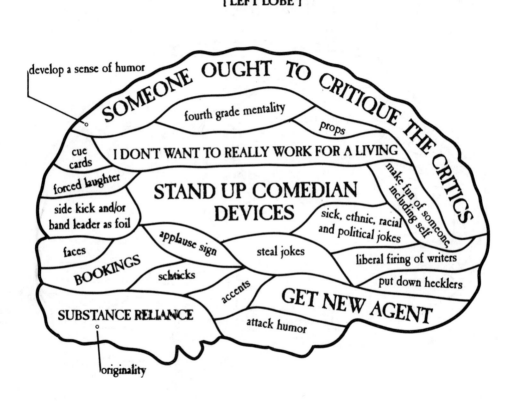

develop a sense of humor

SOMEONE OUGHT TO CRITIQUE THE CRITICS

fourth grade mentality

props

cue cards

I DON'T WANT TO REALLY WORK FOR A LIVING

forced laughter

STAND UP COMEDIAN DEVICES

make fun of someone, including self

side kick and/or band leader as foil

sick, ethnic, racial and political jokes

faces

applause sign

steal jokes

liberal firing of writers

BOOKINGS

schticks

put down hecklers

accents

GET NEW AGENT

SUBSTANCE RELIANCE

attack humor

originality

A TELEVISION PERSONALITY'S BRAIN
[RIGHT LOBE]

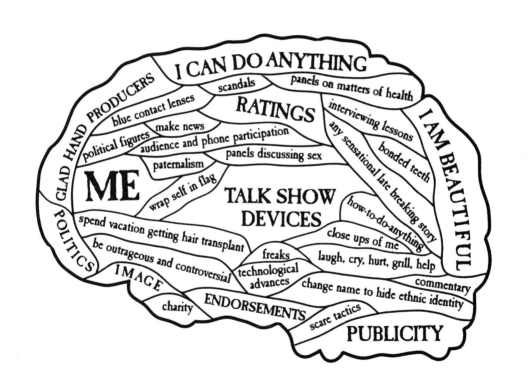

A TENNIS PLAYER'S BRAIN
(LEFT LOBE)

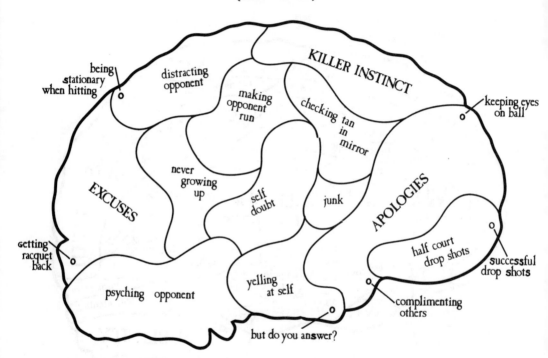

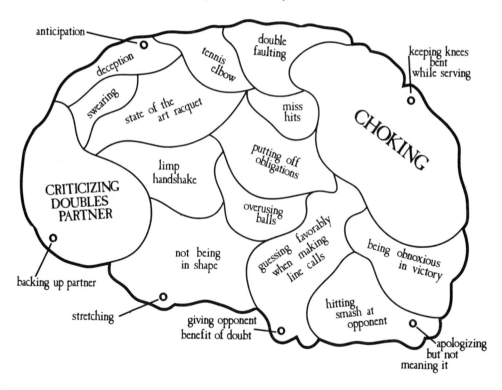

A TENNIS PLAYER'S BRAIN
(RIGHT LOBE)

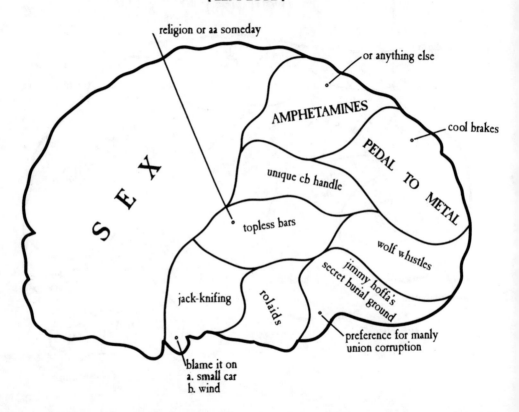

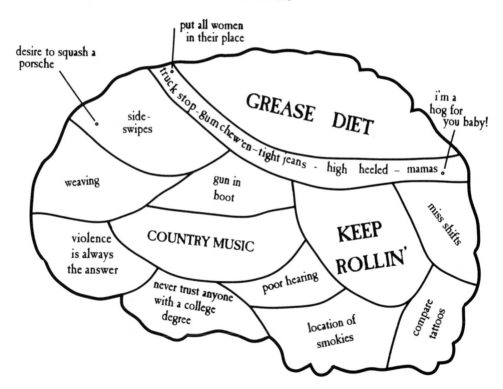

A TV EVANGELIST'S BRAIN

[LEFT LOBE]

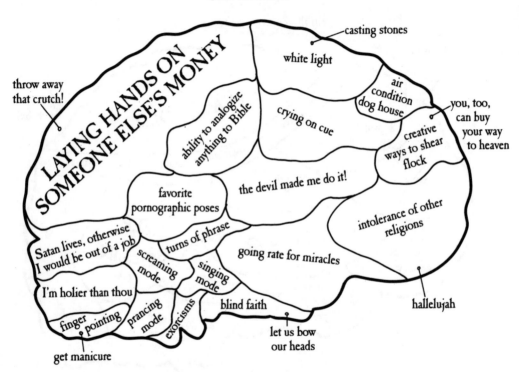

A TV EVANGELIST'S BRAIN

[RIGHT LOBE]

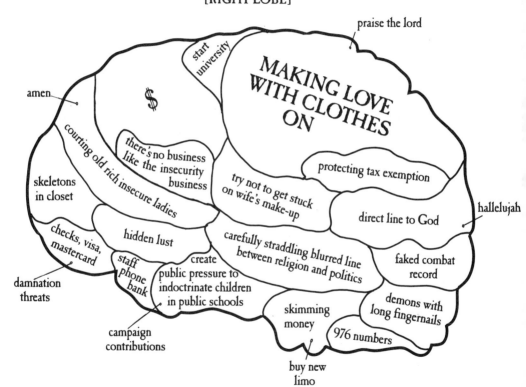

praise the lord

start university

$

MAKING LOVE WITH CLOTHES ON

amen

courting old rich insecure ladies

there's no business like the insecurity business

protecting tax exemption

try not to get stuck on wife's make-up

skeletons in closet

direct line to God

hallelujah

checks, visa, mastercard

hidden lust

carefully straddling blurred line between religion and politics

faked combat record

damnation threats

staff phone bank

create public pressure to indoctrinate children in public schools

skimming money

demons with long fingernails

campaign contributions

976 numbers

buy new limo

A USED CAR SALESMAN'S BRAIN
[LEFT LOBE]

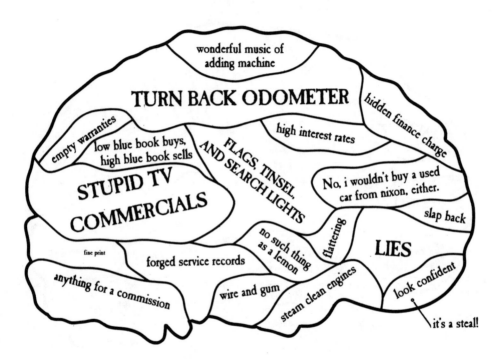

A USED CAR SALESMAN'S BRAIN
[RIGHT LOBE]

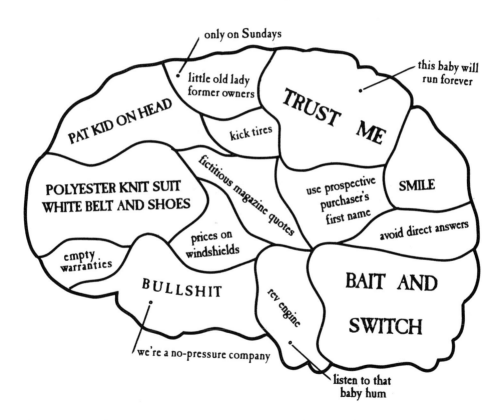

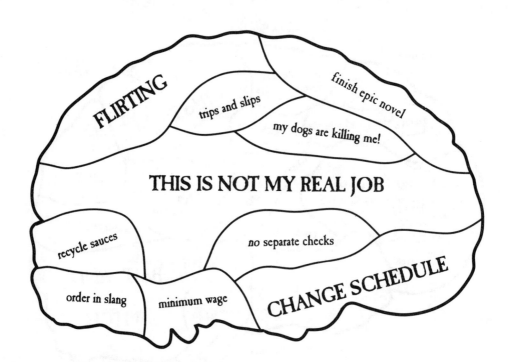

A WAITPERSON'S BRAIN
[RIGHT LOBE]

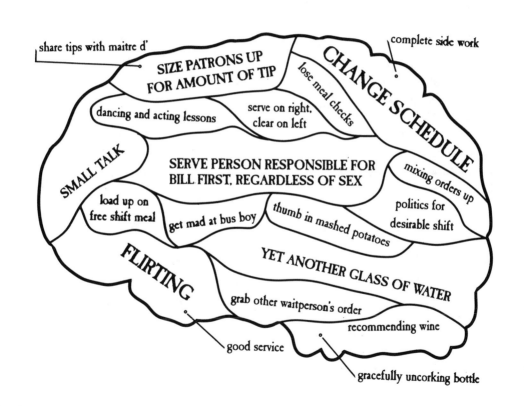

A YUPPIE'S BRAIN
[LEFT LOBE]

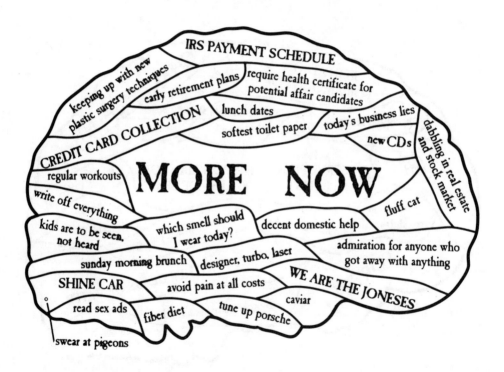

A YUPPIE'S BRAIN
[RIGHT LOBE]

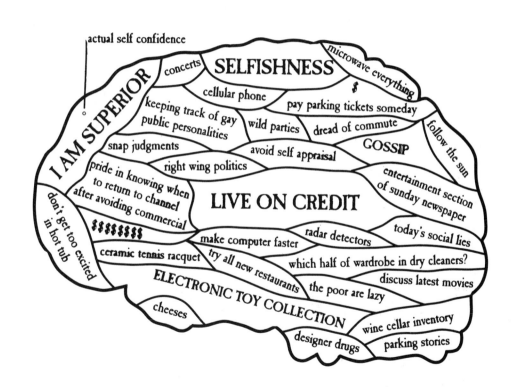

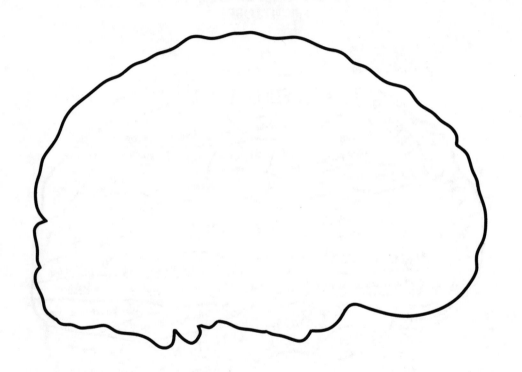

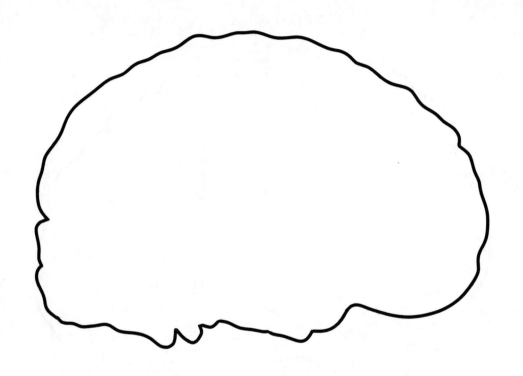

DEDICATION

Thanx to Sophie, Sam, Kathy, John, Mary Pat, Susan, Andrew and Megan Kagel, Waldo and Meli Cook, Jim Bob McCullough, Frank and Angela Worthlessington, June and Stan Shane, Linda Bob and Jim Bob Herndon, "Big D" Darlyne, Bill and Billy Reed, Perry Gorchov, The officers of the Calistoga Yacht Club, i.e., Commodore John Martin, Vice Commodore M. Dennis Clark, Vice Commodore Gerg Murphy, John, Adele, Azalee and Cerise Bostroem, Susan Ovuka, Gillian Peggy B. Wood, Nancy Cheaney, Tina Davis, Greg Ely, Mike Fallow, Patrick Flynn, Zicky Holston, Ted "The Head" Schroeder, Stephen C. Johnson, Bernard Henry Schulte V, Mo McCray, C Rose, the Napa County Bar Association, Rebecca O'Gorman, Ed and Barbara Wetteland, Robert Stricker, Jamie Sutton, Chuck Sims, Bob Diener, Maxine Sidenfaden, Marta Vacincio, Ed Wallis, Jet, Tom, Morgan and Annie White, Kimberly Williams, Richard "Killer" Kandel, Gary and Mary Kilpatric, David "The Great Spauldini" Spaulding, Geri McCauley, Aprille Pihl, Pat Murphy, Mitz Setlow, Bob Zoglin, George Harris, Larry and Ann King, S. Clay Wilson, Bernie Berleffi, Susanne Chapman, Francine and George Davis, Warren and Kippy Hayward, Wayne Dyer, Hugh Gordon, Jack "The Pigeon" Haskins, Caroline Keller, Jill Braddic, Frau Angela and Herr Dr. Mueller, Sandy Gallagher, D.J. Sallee, Lynne Jones, the Ladars, Peggy McCullough, Gary Skoog, all those I forgot and admire and to all Labrador Retrievers everywhere.

FOR INFORMATION ON HOW YOU CAN RECEIVE A 100% COTTON
T-SHIRT WITH YOUR FAVORITE BRAIN ON THE FRONT AND BACK,
PHONE 800-888-0848 x396